Lemon Parade

Tami Rummel

ISBN: 1503345491
ISBN-13: 978-1503345492

Library of Congress Control Number: 2014921513

CreateSpace Independent Publishing Platform, North Charleston, SC

DEDICATED TO

Pete and Ellen Morley

ACKNOWLEDGEMENTS

With heartfelt appreciation for the team who supported this project from concept to publishing: Kathy Wheeler, writing coach; Brynn Warriner, editor; and Lindsay White, artist.

CONTENTS

Introduction

Leading your own parade sounds fun. Easy breezy, like winning the Michigan Lottery or Reader's Digest Sweepstakes. No gimmicks or strings attached. Just check your winning numbers or open your front door, and collect your grand prize with hoopla and jubilation. Like all hometown parades, you expect oodles of free candy, tacky floats, determined musicians, and fire trucks, too. One grand marshal, two tractors, and five proud horses. It's all for one, one for all—the American dream come true with a zesty lemon twist.

My lemon parade is a year focused on faith and fitness. A season of life that was unanticipated, yet treasured. More zest than pith, more positive than negative, more genuine than complicated. Ultimately, more than I ever could have imagined. It was a year that propelled me into meaningful change and new habits. I am an optimist, hard worker, and overachiever. I realize people deal with change all the time, more change than not. I'm not sharing my story to announce a new, sparkly parade route to manage personal or professional change. What I am offering is practical insight into a year of discomfort, development, and experiments.

If you've ever experienced turbulence, upset, or uneasy days, my lemon parade may offer you a hopeful, zesty idea or two. I invite you into my sabbatical year and believe the concepts I experienced will stick with you and benefit you on the day you least expect. During times of significant change, it is often the little things that matter most. Short phrases seemed to spring up continually during my year of personal exploration, and I found that I could easily digest short phrases and use them as my anchors to believe and achieve. I discovered that when life hands you lemons, you need to decide if you will sit back and squeeze the moment or step up and seize the moment. I chose to seize the moments of my lemon-parade year and captured some of them for you. I refer to them as lemon zest. Phrases

1

that inspire you when you need inspiration the most. You can think of them as sweet nuggets or threads of grit running through my story. Lemon zest is an element of surprise that changes the flavor of your daily experiences. I captured many at the end of each chapter and categorized them in the appendix at the end of this book for a quick reference.

The results of my lemon parade have been remarkable. I've achieved four out of my top five goals as this book goes to print. By sharing my story, I hope women everywhere will discover and develop their potential. For twelve months, I invested my time to rebuild my wishbone into a backbone. None of it was easy, but it was all doable.

Chapter One:
What If

As I approached my fiftieth birthday in 2013, I was feeling confident and secure about how my life story would go based on how deeply I cared about my work. I was successful and optimistic. My career path with the American Cancer Society felt more like a privilege than a job for eleven and a half years. It was a synergy of business strategy, measureable goals, compassion, and teamwork that kept my engine burning with love for my job day in and day out. You name it, I had it. The incredible cancer survivors, families, staff, researchers, and donors I interacted with filled me with the ideal mix of challenge and reward. The work fed my naturally competitive spirit, and I believed that by working together, we could defeat cancer. The disease was a gnarly opponent, complex and daunting. All of us were on one big, bold team united against a disease that touches most families. My family was no exception.

Cancer reached its ugly claw into my life in 2010 and quickly took my oldest sister, Kay. Within six weeks, she went from enjoying life as an active mom and grandma with a sudden harsh cough to a seriously ill woman with inoperable, late-stage lung cancer with seven metastatic brain tumors. My concept of all of us versus cancer took a terrible beating that summer.

Defeating cancer was on my mind 24/7/365, and my body knew it. I struggled with the unfairness and randomness of it all. My sister was in her fifties, in the best physical condition of her life, and poof. Harsh cough, biopsy, oncologist, palliative care, last conversation by phone, and then her funeral. It was life-changing and heartbreaking. Nine weeks later our mom died of a sudden stroke at the post office while mailing a birthday card to a friend. The sudden loss of two cool women was very real and too heavy in my little world. During my mom's funeral, we learned my husband's brother was facing a serious cancer diagnosis too. They say bad news comes in sets of three, and it sure did for us that summer.

I needed, and requested, three weeks of family medical leave from work after my mom's death. My heart was broken, and for the first time I felt cancer was going to beat my family and me. The fact of the matter is that I needed more time off to process my grief from these sudden deaths. But instead, I did what I always do when I feel uneasy. I found comfort in lifelong habits and poured myself back into my work. Jim, my husband, encouraged me to get right back into my daily routine. He was verbal about it and firmly believed the best way to manage grief was to carry on like normal. Go back, do your thing, help others, and produce. I knew my marching orders very well. I believed.

I absorbed the concept that it was time for me to put my big girl pants on and push through. My grief was foggy and heavy. I remember thinking to myself, "Why not just lean deeper and harder into work where you thrive, feel alive, and find purpose?" Working full time, while buried in personal grief, seemed to be a convenient and sociably acceptable distraction.

Shortly after returning to work, I learned that the local office of the American Cancer Society where I served as executive director would close in the first few weeks of 2011. Our jobs weren't ending, just being shifted to home offices or regional service centers with moderate changes in roles and responsibilities. Ten area offices had already consolidated that year in Michigan and Indiana, so the news was unsettling but not unexpected.

I added to my grief pile the reality of my rock-solid staff team splitting into multiple locations, and I plowed in deeper. I was determined to make our move and consolidation process as efficient and effective as possible. I had tasks, and tasks had me. I was busy, helpful, determined, and focused.

For Jim and me, the next couple of years were a flurry of change, activity, highlights, and lowlights. My husband retired from his leadership role with the American Red Cross, his father passed away peacefully in his mid-nineties, our neighborhood was hit by a destructive tornado in March 2012, and my role at work continued to change and expand. If there was a top-ten list for major life adjustments, we were checking the boxes like ninja warriors. Each major life change seemed to creep through our marriage like a chronic infection of unrest.

We were good at accommodating and keeping all the balls in the air. Or maybe it is more accurate to say I got really good and really large at it. I slowly crept up, from a size 8 when I started with the American Cancer Society in 2002, to a sedentary size 2xl in 2013. I was starting to feel slightly out of breath when climbing stairs or walking the dogs. Yet I didn't have any concerns about my lifestyle choices at that point. I loved my work and really wanted to fight back against cancer. I had a mission, and the mission had me. You know the saying *Do what you love and never work a day in your life?* I had that. I can testify that loving your work is real and good. And now I know that breaking up with your work is hard, but doable.

The largest wave of restructuring hit my work world in the summer of 2013 when all American Cancer Society staff roles across the country expired, and new job postings were rolled out in month-by-month phases. It was a time of remarkable uneasiness. All staff were encouraged to apply outside, or within the organization, for any role they were qualified to fulfill. Had it been available, I would've wanted the role I was in at the time. It was a great fit and was fulfilling a cutting-edge purpose. But my role, like all others, had a designated expiration date. As you know by now, my go-to response to cope with significant change is to work harder, longer, faster. But this time, that strategy seemed lame given the magnitude of the national change.

Yet, I never felt defeated. I felt confident that Jim and I could figure out a game plan with one good heart-to-heart conversation. We had experience overcoming obstacles, and this was just the next one in the mix. My career had been meaningful. I had been adaptable and resilient with ten supervisor changes in eleven successful years. I could ride this wave too and come out on top. I was a thriving professional with much more to give. I had years of experience, a heart the size of Montana, and enough passion to find the answers.

In my heart, I knew I needed to talk and strategize with someone I trusted, who loved me and knew how much I loved my work. Given the level of uproar within the company at that time, it seemed to take five business days plus weekends to do the work, search for your next role, and prepare for interviews within the organization all at the same time. One close friend reminded me that people who work in nonprofits are used to being stretched thin. He said, "This is beyond thin. This is insane." Weekdays flowed into weekends like work flowed into life. It was one wild river ride, and I needed an anchor.

Those feelings inspired me to launch our fateful Saturday morning conversation, in mid-June 2013. I gathered up my stack of American Cancer Society job postings, time-sensitive work projects, interview prep documents, and one blank sheet of paper into my arms. Next, I asked my anchor for some help—I yelled upstairs and asked Jim to please take a break and join me on the back porch.

The majority of the time, I am a pristine-desk kind of gal. Whether I'm working in a public office or my home office, I have no piles, no random papers—I file and I sort. I believe in handling every document only once. My system of organization works 99.9 percent of the time and enables me to manage a robust quantity of work and volunteer projects.

So you can imagine, my haggard piles and I were enough to quickly grab Jim's attention when he got to the table on the back porch. After one look, he knew this wasn't going to be a simple to-do-list-meets-momentary-overload kind of chat.

Helpful to me was the fact that Jim was very familiar with the American Cancer Society's reorganization model led by a national consulting company. He'd just experienced five years of the same process with the American Red Cross. It was all familiar business within the Rummel household. I believed that all I really needed was a chance to share out loud, hear a little clarity, and a build a joint plan to move us onward and upward. I needed Jim's help and support to decide what jobs to continue applying for, which job offers to potentially accept, what geographic area to consider for our family if we decided to sell our home and relocate again. Decisions were imminent, and opportunities were all over the place.

As a couple, Jim and I had dedicated twenty-eight years of our marriage to serving the missions of the nation's two largest voluntary healthcare nonprofits. Both of us were raised with Midwestern work values, and we're dedicated to professional achievement. Jim lost his mother to cancer in the 1980s, so the fight was personal for him, too. I was confident we could put our heads together and come up with a plan. I felt confident that we could find a niche in the new national operating model for my skills and passion. All we needed to do was prioritize our options of Michigan or Indiana as work locations. Nonprofit organizational restructuring had been a part of our world for eight years, so I knew we could cut to the heart of this conversation.

I asked Jim if we could start our conversation with a blank sheet of paper just to clear and free my mind. I had done that a few years back during a meeting at a hospital when we needed everyone's fresh ideas and buy-in. It worked really well for that group of invested partners, and I thought it was worth a try. We had content overload and needed more white space. I had pages of conference-call notes and job postings on the patio table. What I really needed was something fresh and creative to spark my energy.

We agreed to draw two columns on the blank paper. I titled column one "Indiana" and column two "Michigan." We started listing steps in the Indiana column like selling our home, finding a temporary apartment for me, and relocating to the Hoosier State. My job at the time was facilitating university account teams in Michigan and Indiana to expand and enhance mission and income potential. The staff in Indiana were eager and receptive to campus integration, and spending more time with them was extra appealing.

Jim and I had relocated before for my work when we moved to the Ann Arbor area for my role with the American Cancer Society in 2004. Moving seemed familiar and doable. Column two was for brainstorming opportunities in Michigan: we listed our favorite cities in the state, options for where we might want to live, places family and friends could easily visit, and what type of job was posted for those areas. We agreed that if we were going to relocate for work within Michigan, we needed to be in a town as cool as Ann Arbor, or near one of the big lakes.

I remember thinking this was an odd exercise, but not too odd, considering the reorganization going on with all my colleagues across the country. Some staff had started with their family heart-to-heart conversations as early as February 2013. Hard conversations weren't uncommon in the company culture during the reorg. Jim and I talked about the details of our personal budget and how much we could afford to invest in moving to another state, or a different part of Michigan, to continue my career serving the American Cancer Society.

It felt liberating to talk and dream big. I started to realize the topic had been hanging around my neck for months. Many of my close friends and coworkers were struggling. It was somewhere between surreal and all too real. It started to feel empowering to think strategically and to own my next steps. The plan was blossoming on paper, and I knew by the time we went inside that Jim and I would be on the same page. I would be prepared for solid next steps within the company. I believed.

As we added content to our two columns and talked about our work, dreams, values, time, possibilities, life goals, accomplishments, and priorities, I started to share more and more. Our conversation was spontaneously bubbling up some insightful and encouraging options. Energy was flowing in a good direction. With the spirit of can-do, I shuffled through my piles and found my scribbly "life list," which is like a bucket list. American Cancer Society staff across the country were posting their life lists up on Facebook and celebrating a short list of what they had accomplished so far and what they still wanted to do with their life. The postings were in honor of the Society's one-hundredth birthday that summer. Many people's lists included educational goals, having children, marriage proposals, travel adventures, or endurance events. Earlier that week, while talking to a colleague on the phone, I jotted down my own life list.

As I pulled out my life list, Jim said, "Is there a third column?" I remember crinkling up my forehead and nose like I do when I am confused and said, "What's a third column?" Imagine my optimistic, overachiever, organizer brain trying to understand what on earth a third column is.

I said, "Do you mean a third state to consider? Should I start looking for an American Cancer Society job in another state?" I guess Virginia makes sense because that is where our daughter, Jess, lives. I had looked at postings in Michigan and Indiana only, because that was the region I worked in; that was my territory and my comfort zone. We were so close to a resolution with our happy, two-column paper. What the heck does a third column have to do with any of this right now? Then he said, "A third column to consider. Another option, another choice." Bewildered, I played along. I added another line on the sheet of paper and curiously asked, "What in the world should we title the third column?"

Jim said, "Let's title it What IF?"

"What IF *what*?" I asked.

Right then, for the first time in a very long time, I stopped. I stopped and looked at the three columns. Two filled in with logical next steps. The third one empty. I stared. I felt a little small and a little big all at once. I felt a zap of mysterious energy in the unknown space of the third column. Like a force of unknown potential stirring in my soul. I didn't even know if I wanted anything other than column one or column two. What kind of work does a person do in column three? What kind of identity comes from pure, absolute white space?

Truth be told. All I wanted was the job I was doing at the time with campus engagement. I was happy as a clam developing a university model using American Cancer Society best practices. Building an integrated team. Connecting with passionate volunteers across thirteen campuses from researchers to coaches to students. Impacting fundraising and mission delivery was my happy place. But the reality was that within a few short weeks, that role wouldn't exist anymore. It wasn't available on the new division operating model. I believe the reality of that fact finally hit me in the white space of column three. It was a visual revelation moment for me. I remember thinking, *Courage now would be good*.

My job with the American Cancer Society wasn't hiding in Michigan or Indiana—it was ending. I looked at all three columns with new eyes. I felt all the goodness and comfort of column one and column two. To me those columns were full of potential, projects, answers, deadlines, friends, and colleagues. Then I glanced at column three and it looked white, blank, and empty. I thought to myself, *Is this a goofy life moment when clichés run rampant?* Is this the feeling *When one door closes, a window opens?* Or is this the *When life hands you lemons, you make lemonade* moment? Yes, it is. The good news is that when you get your "What IF" moment, you know it is real and true.

It felt like a whole day had gone by while I was staring at the white space, but in reality just a few seconds later Jim asked, "What goes in column three?" I looked straight down at my draft one-hundredth birthday American Cancer Society life list and wrote all five goals in the "What IF" column. What belonged in my "What IF" column was everything that had been in my heart and on my mind and in my soul, but never mentioned out loud. Not even to Jim, until that moment. These priorities were top of mind for me, but not top of consciousness. What started as a to-do task—to get my life list published on Facebook—became my top five goals for my sabbatical year.

My "What IF" column
1) Live to be one hundred years old
2) Earn a one-year sabbatical
3) Lose fifty pounds
4) Run a 5k with our daughter, Jess
5) Join a church and become active in it

At the bottom of that simple series of five goals, I summed it up in two big, bold words I'd never written down before that moment: faith and fitness.

Jim took one look at the third column and said, "That looks good to me." I smiled and was stunned. It was a moment equivalent to when he said, "Will you marry me?" Our decision was made. A twelve-month sabbatical to focus on faith and fitness inspired by my life list.

How on earth did this happen? What if we hadn't stopped and talked? What if we hadn't started with blank paper? What if I hadn't scribbled down five goals that seemed incredible, but impossible three days earlier? What is on your life list? What is in your heart or in your soul, but not in your vocabulary yet? Grab a sheet of blank paper and share your dreams with someone you trust. It will change your life. It did mine.

Use this white space to list your top five life goals now:

1)

2)

3)

4)

5)

Lemon Zest
   ✓ When life hands you lemons, little things matter.
   ✓ Courage in times of change is good.

✓ At times your work environment is where you thrive, feel alive, and find purpose.

✓ Personal connection to a valuable mission impacts your life in many different ways.

✓ The good news is that when you get your "What IF" moment, you will know it is the truth.

✓ Add your own:

_____

✓ Add your own:

_____

Chapter Two:
Marching Along

Just like those numbing moments of disbelief and joy right after a marriage proposal, I was a bit wobbly the rest of that Saturday. But, I felt a flicker of peace, potential, and prosperity deep in my belly. In hindsight, it was a beautiful day of grace and mercy. After we agreed to move forward with the "What IF" column and focus on achieving my top five goals, it was time to build a plan and work the plan. I believed.

First things first, I wasn't sure how to begin unraveling my life's work, but I did know what my focus would be going forward. It was a gift beyond measure. I had so much to learn about translating work-goal accomplishment into personal-goal accomplishment. I was up for the challenge. The rest of the weekend was quiet, but peaceful.

When Monday morning arrived, I needed to call and update my supervisor. I resigned from my position and opted out of future interviews within the organization. I let go of a role that was concluding at the end of the summer. I was happy to stay on board as long as necessary to help. I didn't have any pressing plans; my top five goals weren't going to shift or change. I was able to connect with staff and volunteers and wrap up pending projects. My final paperwork arrived in an email from the national home office, and my final farewell was eleven weeks after my decision. I remain grateful for that smooth transition. It was productive and valuable time.

One of the hardest phone calls I had to make after the decision was made turned out to be to our daughter, Jess. She is a successful college graduate and savvy businesswoman residing in northern Virginia. It surprised me how emotional I felt sharing my news with her that summer. I felt like a total loser who had failed her life's work and purpose. My identity was so closely tied to my business success that telling Jess I'd chosen to invest in faith and fitness for one year seemed out of order and out of character for me. She was supportive of and confident in my decision.

I experienced waves of grief during my eleven weeks of wrapping up. It was easy to catch myself wishing my role wasn't ending. But sooner rather than later, I had to wrestle with wishing thoughts and decide to focus my energy forward. I decided to recall and connect to the original feeling of the "What IF" column. I had to intentionally practice feeling excitement, potential, and growth. I had to find the ability within my heart to accept the change, be disciplined, and begin to heal.

When I was weak, I worried about feeling alone and feared missing a sense of daily accomplishments. I feared not being part of a team that was making a difference. I feared no opportunity for public speaking and connecting. Another big one was my fear of losing a meaningful message to share. I had absorbed the mission of the American Cancer Society and enjoyed sharing the message with others. I don't know when it went from a job to a lifestyle, but it did. I often mentioned that concept to candidates interviewing for open positions in our Ann Arbor office. Because it was true. This wasn't a job; it was a lifestyle. It was a society of dedicated people pulling in one direction to end a disease that takes so much more than it gives. I was a loyal solider marching along with an army of loyal soldiers.

I needed to develop a strategy to get out in front of my feelings of emptiness and loss. I needed to start trusting the future. I would be fine. I felt like I needed some kind of party or parade to launch my next life chapter. I needed a kick-off, a send-off, an inauguration, or a parade. I had to own my lemon parade. So I did. As I built my plan, short phrases were key to me. The proverbial phrase *When life hands you lemons, make lemonade* really started to resonate with me. It wasn't so much the cheesiness of the saying as it was how long it had been around and how the language was action-oriented. When I would think of that phrase, my head would translate it into something like "When *this* comes your way, do *this*." I thought of children and lemonade stands. It reminded me of the kids' optimism and their desire to make a product, advertise it, and sell it. I needed to keep my plan simple and loud, like a parade. Lots of cheering and lots of energy. All participants moving in the same direction with no end in sight.

Per Wikipedia, the lemon phrase is used to encourage optimism and a can-do attitude in the face of adversity or misfortune. The statement was first penned in a 1915 obit of dwarf actor Marshall P. Wilder. But, the catchy phrase is more often attributed to Dale Carnegie from his 1948 book *How to Stop Worrying and Start Living*. I liked both stories, but especially the use by Mr. Carnegie. His book title seemed appropriate for my next chapter of life. I decided to build my team, get out in front of my situation, make it as festive as a holiday parade, and bring people along for the ride. It was a new day and a new way. I believed.

I was blessed with a huge personal aha moment during my last week of service with the American Cancer Society. I realized I could take all my work experience with me. I didn't have to leave any skills behind. But, I certainly needed to learn some new techniques to build a life of faith and fitness. Those were two areas I had put on the back burner for at least fifteen years, if not longer. Before I could dive into my top five goals, I had to reflect and make an inventory of what was in good shape and what needed to be improved in my life. It was one thing to believe and another to believe in the right stuff. I assumed some of my stuff was out of order.

All of my life, whatever I believed, I believed with all my might. Right or wrong. I believed hard. I lived hard. I worked hard. I wore my toothbrush out hard. I wore my high heels out hard. I wore fountain pens out hard. You name it—even watch batteries—I wore them out hard. My mom taught me life was either this or that. Either right or wrong. Either in or out. Either included or excluded. Either up or down. Either complete or incomplete. I'd been missing my "What IF" column for fifty years, and I needed that element of white space in my life.

I know you've heard the saying *Don't die with your song still in you*. I felt that way about my top five goals. I was going to make sure I didn't die with my "What IF" column in me. It was coming out to play, to breathe, to live, and to start a big, noisy lemon parade. A parade where you investigate life, where you listen, where food tastes different, and where you apply all the principles of business strategy to successful faith and fitness development. A place and time in life where you measure success not in balance sheets or expense reports but in pounds lost and moments of prayer.

Everything started to change for me. I was becoming aware of my surroundings in a new way. I felt like a combination explorer and treasure hunter. Discovery was all around me in sights and sounds. I overhead a song at the grocery store and went home to ask Jim if he knew the words. After hearing it only once, I knew the lyrics included the phrase *525,600 minutes/how do you measure, measure a year.* I'd never heard that song before and had no idea it was from a Broadway production. When I got home, I grabbed a calculator and double-checked. Yup, the song was right. I had 525,600 minutes in my year. Next, I hunted for the song on YouTube. The song seemed to be written for me. I was fully committed to making my year all that it could be. "Seasons of Love" became an anthem for me early in my lemon-parade year. Milestones, short phrases, and mantras were all key components of my evolving space in time.

In the beginning, I needed to know that not only could I march to the beat of my own drum, I could learn to love it as much as I loved my work. Yikes. Imagine that. Could I possibly ever replace the joy and feelings of working with highly motivated volunteers? What could ever fill in the open gaps in my life where team meetings, public speaking, and big community events used to be? How could I ever feel useful, and whom would I connect with as I moved on? So many questions, and so much white space. Mega discomfort was my reality. I believed.

Move on was a short phrase that caught me by surprise. This short phrase was especially tough to digest, because moving wasn't a part of my daily routine at all. No physical movement nor any type of fitness activity. None. No physically demanding hobbies, sports, or passions. Certainly can't count walking two four-year-old Maltese pups as physical anything. They are content walking one loop of our cul-de-sac or one loop around the house. I pretty much depended on my body to simply carry around my brain. But without activity, and with lazy nutrition, my body had swollen from a slender size 8 to a plump size 20 over the course of my tenure with the American Cancer Society.

I had literally put on big girl pants. I didn't even recognize my pants when folding clothes on the dryer. They looked big enough for two people. It didn't happen overnight; the weight took years to accumulate, pound by pound over time. My weight gain was a side-effect of a sedentary, production-oriented lifestyle I had readily adopted. It seemed a fair trade-off for the cost of doing business. Larger clothes are widely available, gaining weight beyond your ideal frame isn't illegal, and no one really calls you out for it. People had called me out for being an overachiever for years, but no one called me out for being an overeater. Ever.

As a creative, passionate, goal-oriented, "can do well" gal, it seemed the more lemons showed up in my life the busier I became and the heavier I became physically, mentally, and spiritually. Over a decade, I slowly grew to a tight size 20. I remember feeling okay about that because there was still size 3X to grow into, and I believed I would get there, too. That is embarrassing to say now, but at the time it was acceptable to me. It was like a trade-off. Do what you must to keep producing excellent work.

Strange realities hit me when I turned in my laptop, office keys, contact list and was facing life without a job for the first time since I was thirteen years old. A scary reality was not having health insurance. Quickly, the thought of being uninsured became a motivator: if I don't have insurance to cover illness, I'd better get well. I started to own and build my wellness plan out of necessity, and I felt inspired. When your dreams and courage are greater than your fears, life makes sense. I had some white space and unknowns, but I had determination. Knowing I had the courage to leap into the "What IF" column was a difference maker for me. I knew I had every skill I needed to achieve my top five goals. Once my heart, brain, soul, and ambition aligned, I was unstoppable.

I had to define what I needed to feel secure enough to accomplish my goals: I needed to remain in my home for the whole year. I needed to purchase basic health insurance. I needed access to a gym for one year. We budgeted our sabbatical bank account to fulfill these three needs for 365 days. With these needs covered, and my personal mission statement in hand, I was ready to tackle my top five goals step by step.

When I wrote my personal mission statement sixteen years ago, the task seemed important and relevant to me. I liked that my personal mission statement was simple and easy to remember. I tucked the statement in a file folder and basically kept it there, safe and sound. My personal mission statement is "To live a genuine life, on purpose with purpose." When I held my personal mission statement up to the third column on that remarkable Saturday with Jim, it was the resounding final exclamation point. I promise you, if you craft a personal mission statement now, the day you need it most, it will matter most.

My faith and fitness development plan included putting myself in uncomfortable situations at least once a week. I knew my desire to learn and live during my lemon-parade year was bigger than my fear, so I faced my insecurities head on. One Friday morning, I went to the gym to attend a water Pilates class. What makes that so uncomfortable? I didn't know anyone, and I'd never done Pilates, let alone a water Pilates class. I didn't own an attractive swimsuit because I had avoided beachwear for years. All I had was a goofy, two-piece swimsuit with the floppy tank top that barely covered up my size 20+ body. It certainly wasn't athletic wear. I arrived at the small, warm pool twenty minutes early, which cracked me up. I am so responsible, I can't even show up late for something I dread. Humor is helpful during discomfort.

I arrived at the pool feeling insecure and wanting to be invisible. But as fate would have it during my lemon-parade year, a beautiful, friendly woman was already in the pool eager to chat. My first thought was *Maybe she isn't friendly and won't do anything but smile.* So I am thinking and wishing, please, lady, just smile and let me be lonely all alone. I can do this. Oh please, Lord, don't let her talk to me. Please. I prayed that quick, simple prayer, and boy-oh-boy did God have a different plan for my brokenness in the pool that day.

Oh no. She is coming to my corner of the warm pool before I even get in. She is going to talk to me. Imagine this scene. I am a professional fundraiser, community networker, my entire life has been focused on starting vibrant conversations and engaging complete strangers, and all I wanted to do was evaporate. Please evaporate me right now, God. I prayed again. I can't stand this. Except I had to. I had to start new habits. This was going to be incredibly uncomfortable, and I needed it. I needed it to build my internal and external confidence. I also had a mantra that was very helpful during the first few weeks of my lemon parade. It helped me to repeat over and over in my mind, "I am confident in my decision."

Here came the beautiful woman, here I was feeling exposed with my mantra blaring in my brain. She swam right up next to me and said, "Hi, My name is Fran. What is your name, and what do you do?"

All I heard is, "What do you do?" And the lump in my throat crushed my mantra. I said, "I don't know."

Blank time and space. "For the first time in my life, I don't know what I do. I was a fundraiser for the American Cancer Society, but I'm not that anymore." Tears welled up in my eyes, to match the lump in my throat and goose bumps on my arms, and she didn't flinch. She stood there as the absolute pillar of strength I needed. She was confident, kind, and friendly. I saw a reflection of my true self in her spirit at that exact moment.

I felt like my right thumb and index finger were making a giant "L" sign over my forehead and that time had stopped. Me, in the pool, in my ugly swimsuit, without water shoes, and with tears. Lumps in my throat and on my hips. Courage now would be good.

Instead of backing off or sliding away, the beautiful woman firmly took my hand and told me point blank, "You will be FINE!" I hadn't even noticed the pool had filled up with at least ten women of all ages during my time warp. All I know is that lovely woman literally took me by the hand and told me I would be fine and deep, deep, deep down in my heart, I believed her.

From that day on, I had more stamina and faith as I put myself into unknown, uncomfortable environments, and they always turned out to be growth moments. Each new circumstance felt necessary, and I never felt alone. Fran taught me to leap forward and to trust.

God started placing people along my lemon-parade route who were strong in faith and vibrant in their determination to help others. Blessings flowed in all directions from that day forward. I felt His presence, and I decided to open every portal of my soul to learn His way. I was a humble, happy student of life.

Fran and I exchanged phone numbers in the locker room, and I honestly thought that whoever she was, she made a huge impact on my lemon parade and my life's journey, but that day was it. That was sweet, and it was a one-time thing. She told me I would be fine, and I believed. How could there be more?

But there was much more to come. The next morning, my phone rang, and I could see it was Fran's number. It was great, but startling, to hear her voice. My heart was hoping she was calling to remind me that I would be fine. That would have been more than sufficient. Just tell me one more time, and I am good. I am a quick learner: Tell me once, and I get it. Tell me with passion, and I believe it.

Rather than telling me that, Fran jumped right in and told me that she had gone home and told her husband, Ed Coy, all about me. My brain zipped into overdrive. Wonder what she told Ed? My story seemed a little slim right then. The idea of them talking about me cracked me up. Humor was a sweet companion. My imagination convinced me that Fran's conversation with Ed was brief and went something like this: I found a sad woman in the pool today. She seems kind enough and could have some potential, but her heart sure is broken. Fran's voice on the phone pulled me back into the conversation. "Ed and I want to invite you and your husband to join us at church tomorrow. We're always running late, and we sit in the back row. See you there, okay?"

Fran's call, and personal invitation to attend church, was an answer to years and years of Jim's prayers. I felt God's love working in our life more at that moment than ever before. But my thoughts felt unglued. My brain started to zip back into an overdrive of concern about what, how, why, and *Whose life am I living? How do you even get a call like this from a water Pilates class? Is this how my lemon-parade year will go? Will people call me out of the blue? Is this legit? Is this scary? Is this all part of the "What IF" column? Oh my, is this the feeling of white space?*

Knowing I would need to talk to Jim about this call as soon as I hang up, I got my wits about me enough to ask, "What church?" Fran said, "The Methodist church in Dexter." Zip back to my optimistic, overachiever brain. I was raised Catholic; Jim was raised Lutheran. Where does Methodist fit in this plan? Methodist. Dear God, really? How on earth am I going to find my way in this year? Courage now would be good. "Okay, thank you for the invite," I said to Fran. "See you there."

That personal phone call was how the faith part of my lemon parade began. Incredibly beautiful in hindsight; incredibly freaky in real time. When I share that God's hand was in every part of my year, I am not exaggerating. Jim had been asking me to join a church for many years. My response was consistent—and not supportive. I would tell him that my plate was full, my life was full, and I was content doing the good mission work I was doing. My work fulfilled my need to connect in the community. I didn't have enough time, interest, or energy for a church. I remember telling him to go find a church for himself if he felt he needed one. I was fine without.

Looking back, I can think of at least three times over the last ten years when God nudged me to notice His hand in my work. The first time was during a colorectal cancer education program with the Foster Grandparents Group at the Ypsilanti Community Center. The local physician called moments before the program started and told me he was held up with a patient at the hospital and unable to provide the morning's presentation. The colon cancer survivor speaker was with me, and the room was full with nearly one hundred attendees, so we proceeded. I let everyone know I wasn't a physician and that we would go through the slides and share the prevention and early detection information. I did my best to share the slides and remarks, often reminding the audience I was trained to share the content but was not a physician. The group seemed interested and engaged in the topic except for one older woman in the back of the large meeting space whom everyone greeted when they entered the room.

We got through the series of slides and shared the survivor's personal story explaining the importance of early detection. As we packed up and started to exit the room, I walked right by the wise, old woman in the back of the room. I thought she had fallen asleep just five minutes after I started speaking. Much to my surprise, her eyes opened as I walked by and she grabbed my arm with her strong, frail-looking hands. I knelt down and braced myself to hear her feedback because it was clear she was very influential to the group. She pulled me very close and said, "I prayed for you during this entire program because no one has ever discussed this topic with our community. Bless you and thank you." I was dumbstruck and speechless. Here I was assuming she was nodding off and sleeping, and she was calling upon God's mercy to get the information to her people. It was a huge God moment that will stick with me forever. The next thing she said was, "May I kiss you on the cheek before you go?" Oh my, I was getting the blessing of the eldest woman of the group. The experience changed me, but not enough to propel me to church, or to a personal relationship with God, at the time.

Each year, Jim and I walked the high school track during an American Cancer Society fundraising event with a woman who was very passionate and dedicated to the cause. She always told us how she prayed each year for a new pair of white tennis shoes so she could walk the track and not hurt her feet. She believed God would provide for her new shoes if she watched her budget all year long. One thing she really liked was mushrooms in her daily omelet for breakfast. She went without mushrooms ever since she started saving for her shoes. We enjoyed taking her to breakfast after the walk and ordering her a large mushroom omelet in the small town of Eaton Rapids. God was nudging, but I wasn't listening.

The third time I felt His nudge, while working with the American Cancer Society, I finally paid attention. This time came through a poignant phone call with a wise university physician who told me that our feet point forward for a reason. Dr. Aguwa was firm, honest, and forthright with me on the phone. She told me that once we make tough, faithful decisions about our life, we must move on. My ears were finally opened by her short phrase. I felt God's third nudge in her voice on the phone. She told me, "No more tears. You've completed the work that was meant for you to accomplish, now move on and be strong." She spoke with the empathy of a medical professional, a survivor, a physician, and a longtime Society volunteer. I knew her as a faithful servant, and God had sent a messenger that left me no room to hide. I listened, and I believed.

Lemon Zest

✓ Seek and find a source of comfort and peace in your life.
✓ Each new beginning deserves a parade of some sort.
✓ Believing in the right stuff requires courage, discretion, and time.
✓ The day you need it most, your personal mission statement will matter most.
✓ You can recognize your potential in a new Christian friend.
✓ Planned daily discomfort helps create new habits.
✓ Your feet point forward for a reason.
✓ Add your own:

_____

✓ Add your own:

_____

Chapter Three:
Cool Women Show Up

Fear can't touch a moving target is another short phrase that stuck with me during my lemon parade. One of my heroes who models strength, courage, and constant renewal is Eleni Kelakos. She is a professional speaker, actress, author, stunning woman, and dear friend I met eight years ago while working with the American Cancer Society. Meeting her, and becoming a part of her world, was one of the numerous rewards of my community involvement. I met her while making cold calls searching for people with a passion for the issue of breast cancer.

The moment I dialed and heard Eleni's voice, I knew I'd met a soul sister. Within days, she was at my office with a yellow legal pad penning a song she would compose and perform for our local volunteers. Eleni, like most people you meet, had loved ones affected by cancer, and she had a desire to use her talent to layer goodness on top of badness. We built an instant partnership of cool-women power. Being in her presence is like putting on your very own superhero cape and flying high. She believes in dreaming big. Within months of writing her song for the volunteers of the American Cancer Society, she was performing it at our local Relay For Life volunteer summit. Soon after that, she was facilitating our speakers bureau training. Memories of observing gifted people like Eleni share time and talents with cancer survivors and their caregivers will stick with me forever.

During my lemon-parade year, I reached out to Eleni with a personal handwritten note asking if I could join one of her professional public speaking workshops and serve as her sidekick. One of my sabbatical objectives was to be connected to leaders and learners. I felt a strong desire to invest my time soaking up the energy of people who give of themselves to make tomorrow better for others.

Eleni received my note with her brave heart wide open and said she had never been approached with a similar offer. She was intrigued. Eleni reached out to me the week prior to my sidekick debut and asked if I wanted to present a three-minute speech along with the workshop participants. Huge, instant lemon moment for me. My immediate thoughts were questions: *How would that work? What is my topic? I left my topic behind. I don't know what my next topic is yet. Can't I just observe and sidekick in silence?* Silence would work, because I don't have a prepared message anymore.

But, I do have a "What IF" column and my top five goals. The opportunity to prepare a message and speak in public again felt yummy and delightful. "Oh, yes!" I replied. I knew my topic had to be relevant. Eleni's criteria for the public speaking workshop was that we must be passionate, knowledgeable, and convincing about our topic. The topic I was most passionate about was my personal sabbatical. How does a person grab her dream and then live it without remorse, regret, or guilt? How does that work? I was just starting to get a glimpse of the realization that not knowing all the answers doesn't mean I'm unsuccessful.

On the day of Eleni's workshop, I was pumped up. I knew my role. I arrived early. I felt abundant success brewing in the room, along with fresh coffee. I was hosting, solving simple logistics problems, offering nametags, prepping the refreshments, you name it. I loved it. I was a real sidekick. I felt as happy as can be.

I knew what I was passionate about. I had prepared my three-minute speech and bought my lemon. Everyone showed up eager to learn. We were all nervous to be critiqued and eager to be better public speakers by the end of the day. I was a living specimen in a tender, vulnerable transition from professional, to observer, to sidekick, to presenter once again. I was everything and nothing at the same time. It was safe, familiar, good, and new all bundled into one day. Life was real and surreal—again.

When it was my turn, I presented my lemon-parade story in three minutes. I shared my dream and my reality in one hundred eighty seconds. In Ann Arbor, with Eleni and her students, my story found its first audience of believers. The supportive look on Eleni's expressive face transformed my year from a science experiment to a personal mission trip. What I needed that day was a chance to share my story in a safe, collaborative public learning environment. I got what I needed and more. I learned that it is pivotal to connect yourself to trusted professionals during times of significant personal transformation. Quality matters. Get yourself to the best if you want to become the best.

The men and women in Eleni's training instantly understood and supported my message with their whole hearts, minds, and souls. They didn't even know me. But they knew my story. The truth is that life hands people lemons all the time. There really isn't anything new under the sun. It might not be fair, or logical, but it happens all the time. They all knew the concept of making lemonade. Of taking the lemon situation and making it into something sweeter. What inspired them was my determination to do it with faith and fitness as the focus. They wanted more. They wanted to hear how someone finds the courage to stop, seek discomfort, and include others in the process. They wanted more of the spirit it takes to get out in front of your mess, own it, and make it a lemon parade.

That day I knew for a fact that I hadn't lost my purpose or my passion. They were expanding, not shrinking. I showed up complete and whole. I learned that sweaty palms, nervous-stomach butterflies, and sharing myself in front of a group to make a difference wasn't over for me at all—it wasn't in the past. I knew in my soul that the best was yet to come for me. It was three minutes of faith and fitness. Discipline and hope. Belief and action.

The sidekick role rocked my world. Before the lunch break, after we each made our speech, I was in the tiny kitchen adjacent to the meeting space folding salami into attractive triangles, tossing salad, and listening. It was peaceful and purposeful. I was fully present in the moment, doing my thing. I knew it was all going to be okay. My lemon parade had found its first group of advocates and champions. Every time I stretched, I went farther, faster. Discomfort and risk were my new best friends.

At the end the workshop, we cleaned up the meeting space and debriefed. Eleni shared that she had been on the road all week traveling from here to there and all points in between supporting clients. She explained how much my presence had boosted her energy and focus that day. As if I were the gift of the day when in reality, I was the receiver of the gift. The reality is that relationships with talented, vibrant people aren't linear; they are full-circle. Unbroken, full-circle relationships are critical components of life and of learning how to prevail. At least once per month, I had to be in the presence of a real leader. I need the teacher, mentor, learner thing and I found it to be mutually beneficial. It was a day full of lemon-zest moments that changed me and added remarkable flavor to my life. Moments you never forget are zesty and golden.

Lemon Zest
- ✓ Fear can't touch a moving target. —Eleni Kelakos
- ✓ Lemon zest is an element of surprise that changes the flavor of your day.
- ✓ Not knowing doesn't equal being unsuccessful.
- ✓ Life hands people lemons all the time.
- ✓ Relationships with talented, cool, vibrant people aren't linear; they are full-circle.

✓ Every time you stretch, you will go farther, faster.
✓ Add your own:

_____

✓ Add your own:

_____

Chapter Four:
Do It Afraid

Seizing an opportunity to own your time is essential to lemon-parade success. The amount of time you grab can vary from an hour, a week, a month, to a year. Owning, planning, and managing your time to achieve personal goals, big or small, is empowering and possible. I believe women everywhere must stop and own their potential. Transforming business skills into life skills is hard, but doable with clear choices and discipline. You can transform your wishbone into a backbone. Move your thoughts from wishing and wanting to being and doing. Strength to create change comes from within—one choice at a time. It really is that simple.

I thrived in the work environment of the American Cancer Society for countless reasons, but one that continues to inspire me is the organization's dedication to measureable income goals balanced with professional competencies. The standards were based not only on hitting the numbers, but also in how you got the work done. A person's attitude, behavior, and conduct were a percentage of the formula for evaluation and success.

One competency that was top of mind for me at all times was a "can do" attitude. I remember when my first supervisor did my annual review, and I received the equivalent of a B+ in "can do" attitude. It was not the grade I expected or desired on my annual review—or report card ever for that matter. I prefer an A+ in "can do." I decided I needed to do a better job demonstrating my "can do" spirit. So I did. Once the mind decides, the body follows. Can do. Will do. *Will* demonstrate *can do*. It was a helpful leadership mantra for me and enabled me to always find a way to get the job done.

The fabric of my life became stronger with every supervisor I had during my American Cancer Society career. Ten supervisor changes in eleven years gave me the chance to demonstrate "can do" in ten different ways. Constant change helped me own my personal and professional outcomes. Interacting with smart, dedicated, successful overachievers on a daily basis was nourishing and made my heart go "thump" at work. They were my tribe of choice. I was part of a huge crew of staff and volunteers relentlessly striving to do more. To always do more. They affected my DNA in a good way, because it was acceptable to dream big and stretch the boundaries of creative, good works.

My challenge was to apply what I know about successful business goal setting and achievement to my personal goals of faith and fitness. How do I build, and work, a plan that transforms my weight and physical ability? I started by picking apart what elements made me love my job. I became my own coach and servant leader. It was brilliant.

As long as I can remember, I've used a four-step method to manage my calendar and goal achievement. I used that same plan to guide my faith and fitness goals. I think of this as a full circle of how work gets done—Plan, Do, Review, and Improve. The important part is not to skip any step. Jumping right from planning to doing and back again is tempting. It's always better to complete the four steps, catch opportunities in the review process, and improve the plan as you go. I use this daily, weekly, and monthly to make progress. It works for business, and it works for faith and fitness development, too.

Figure 1: How Work Gets Done

Knowing that one of my goals was to become a slimmer, fitter 5k runner, I needed to learn the basics and do what runners do. I needed to make a conscious shift from wishing my happy life hadn't changed to building an identity rooted in faith and fitness. I knew this reinvention was possible. I set my mind and started on the personal plan to last me another fifty great years. Living to be one hundred years young was another of my top five goals. My paternal great-grandmother, Josephine Tamblyn, was ninety years young when I was born. She lived for a noble one hundred four years. I have the genetic potential to be a centenarian and plan to get there.

"Learner" is one of my dominant personality traits, and I knew I would need a guide or resource to get started with running. I reached out to a friend who had started running, and she recommended I pick up a copy of *Run Your Butt Off* by *Runner's World* magazine. Well that sounded just right for me, because the title made me chuckle, and I had a butt that needed to be off sooner rather than later. Being optimistic and resourceful were pillars of my lemon-parade year.

Personal development has been a lifelong passion of mine. Primarily, I've studied leadership to improve my business skills. Titles on developing leaders, servant leadership, and applying Christian values to business strategies line my bookshelves. Now was the time for me to apply leadership strategy to my faith and fitness development, and I approached it as my fulltime job. My plan included the freedom to discover new skills while retaining lessons I'd learned along the way. No doubt in my mind this would build my strong mental, physical, and spiritual backbone. The truth is you don't have to give up your history to reinvest in yourself. I learned to value my past experiences while refining and adding new experiences to my toolkit.

I began filling my lemon-parade route with knowledge and inspired people, while keeping out clutter. I decided to appreciate every new challenge and push back fear. Learning that fear was a deal-breaker and energy zapper for me was key. I learned that each time I felt fear, it was a test. By transforming my wishbone to a backbone, I became confident in my strength to conquer the feeling of fear and, as Joyce Meyer boldly says, "Do it afraid."

I agree with Joyce but decided for me, doing it afraid *with others* was essential. I asked my sister Connie if she would go with me to buy my first Bible. It was a big milestone day, and I knew she would help me find one that was just right for me. I knew I needed her help, and I wasn't afraid to ask. Jim had several Bibles in our home, but I needed my own. I felt compelled to own my relationship with God and His Word. I believe in action. By leaning on God, I slowly built a solid foundation, and the broken parts of my heart started to heal. Peace of mind is His promise.

When fearful thoughts bombarded me, I called on my new skill set to push those feelings to the side. Recognizing fear and doubt as unwanted obstacles allowed me the opportunity to practice and discipline my mind.

One of the essential benefits of seeing physical changes in my body as I exercised and lost weight was the response I got from family and friends. What I learned was that when people share their observations of your weight loss, you can remind yourself that in order to change your physical condition, you had to change your discipline, your habits, and your thought process. It was validating for me on multiple levels. Their comments were external proof that my internal plan was working. Hearing their honest comments linked progress to the review portion of my simple model of how work gets done. Weighing myself once a month on the scale at the gym was another measurement. As was my favorite measurement: shopping for new pants that fit my new, smaller self.

Stepping on the scale was one of my early signs that this path was blessed and necessary for me. About twelve years ago, my sister Kay abruptly asked me how much I weighed at a family holiday gathering. I had just had my annual physical so I told her I weighed 157. She said, "No way." Her cardiologist had just told her that she needed to drop fifty pounds or face imminent open-heart surgery. She weighed 207 pounds that day. She didn't drop the weight as her doctor suggested. Kay did end up having open-heart surgery and, eventually, terminal cancer.

I weighed 207 when I started at the gym. That fact was unsettling, and I felt forewarned by my sister. I tried not to get fixated on the numbers during my lemon-parade year, but I measured pounds lost and tracked it as a motivator. You can see my tracking tool in Appendix One. You'll see that during the first months, the weight dropped off at a pound per week. That was inspiring. But once it slowed down, then it was absolute focus and discipline. It came off slowly, but never went back on.

Pants size was another big indicator for me, and I really enjoying donating my pants as the size dwindled from 2x to XL to large to medium to a size 10, then the infamous pair of size 8 capris in the summer. I did take a picture of the first size 8 tag from the black capri pants I bought ten months into my lemon parade. I posted the picture on Facebook. It was a visual sign of progress and commitment to my plan. I saved the size 8 tag in my jewelry box. Celebrating milestones matters. Lemon-parade thoughts focus on accepting today, moving on, and celebrating what will be, with cool people cheering the whole route.

Beyond pant size, combining faith and fitness milestones was significant for me. I knew from past business experience that feeling a big win within the first ninety days of my lemon-parade year was necessary. It worked out that we completed the new member class at our church in mid-November 2013. The Sunday service, when we formally joined the church, was just four days before Thanksgiving Day. My first 5k was on Thanksgiving morning. I suggest you plan a public, spiritual, deeply personal expression of your faith and fitness commitment within the first ninety days of your journey. That week publicly galvanized my commitment to God, family, friends, and myself. I was speechless at church and emotional at the run. Positive emotions are signs that you are firing on all cylinders. I was remaking a good woman into a great one.

Each day going forward, I used personal and professional disciple to manage flickers of disappointment or concern that came my way. I simplified this for Jim one day and told him, "I am learning to manage my angst." Rather than getting caught up in regrets, what-ifs, or angst, I intentionally redirected my energy into positive, backbone-building strength through prayer and confidence.

As my to-do list changed, I decided it was time to work on my to-be list. Changing my perspective one step at a time was a conscious choice and an excellent exercise for my self-discipline. I knew I was committed to twelve months of self-development and discovery, and I wanted to be a rock star at my sabbatical year. The ability to be thoughtful with my whole brain was inspiring and intriguing. I began tracking key points on notes jotted down in random places, sticky notes, pieces of paper in my purse. I had a glimmer of what life without the day-to-day rush of a packed calendar could feel like. Words filling my to-be list at the very beginning included potential, desire, talent, options, significance, happy, observant, tuned in, present, sensitive, and fully alive.

What if you stop now to begin your to-be list? Even if it has be written down next to your to-do list? What if the purpose of my sabbatical was to share this thought and inspire others to love and depend on their personal to-be list as much as their powerful to-do list?

The start of my to-be list
To be able to let a dream come true
To feel lighter
To be lighter
To be wiser
To be available to the Holy Spirit
To be the mum, wife, sister, friend I had dreamed of being if given the time
To be the best version of myself
To be just enough
To be okay with being unclear about what the future holds
To be able to put off something until tomorrow
To be confident in my decision to live the dream
To be able to live one year without the joy of work
To be known as a Christian woman who trusts in God
To be okay when the year ends

At Thanksgiving time, I realized goal achievement was a way to glorify God. I learned faith isn't something you learn, model, or absorb. It is something you practice. One decision at a time. One decision at a time to pray first. To lean on God is a good thing. He expects that much conversation with us, and He cares about the little things of our lives. He cares about our priorities and wants to be our number one. Learning that I could build a personal go-to relationship with God through prayer required discipline and grace. The mercy to remind and gently correct myself during times of personal tests strengthened my "faith muscles."

It would take me twelve months of daily discipline to remember to always pray first. It was a new habit, and new habits take time. Old habits die hard. But they do die. All my life, I'd used a self-reliant, five-step model of getting stuff done: Step 1) Understand the need or problem; Step 2) Make a plan to fix or solve the issue; Step 3) Work the plan; Step 4) Work the plan hard; and Step 5) Work the plan harder. Repeat as often as necessary.

Before my lemon parade, I failed to pause and listen for His plan or His guidance as a first step. I marvel at how many times I unconsciously insulted God with all my hard work. I thought He was up there in Heaven and I was down here on Earth. I learned about prayer in my women's Bible-study group, from a personal coach, and also from remarkable women who became mentors of my prayer life. Prior to these groups, I hadn't listened to people share their one-on-one conversations with God. I knew memorized prayer from growing up Catholic. I heard ministers and laypeople pray from the altar, but where I really learned the depths of prayer was at my kitchen table and in coffee shops. I was a student soaking up prayer in unusual places, and that helped me to understand that God is everywhere all the time.

I found it interesting that I had a personal coach for prayer, but not a personal coach for fitness. One great thing about my lemon-parade year was that I didn't judge myself; I just became aware and got help where I needed it most. All through my year of personal transformation, taking one step at a time toward improvement was significant. I remember the first time I walked one mile at a brisk pace on the treadmill without stopping. It was huge. I texted Jess. It took me weeks to achieve that goal. First you walk, then you run. A favorite short phrase that sticks.

One of the things I enjoyed the most about nonprofit management was the never-ending cycle of planning, achieving, celebrating, and starting the meter of goal achievement back to zero each fiscal year. I thrived in an environment that was always ramping up, always measuring, and always starting over. A friend from church said to me, "I would never want to be a fundraiser. I hate asking people for money." I smile when I think about how passionate she was about NOT wanting to do what I love doing. My reply to her was, "The thing about fundraising is you aren't asking for donations for yourself. The professional fundraiser's role is to facilitate the success of the donor and the mission. You are the bridge builder and facilitator of success. You are the steward of the donor dollar. You are responsible for making sure the dollars are properly managed and invested to accomplish necessary goals. Providing that service to the community with confidence is a privilege. Ultimately, you aren't asking for the donor's money; you're facilitating their ability to give and bringing them great joy."

When I shared my perspective on fundraising, I realized it was an alien concept to her. During simple conversations like that, I would discover essential pieces of my lemon-parade puzzle. I would stop and reflect. What can I pull from my experience as a successful professional fundraiser to apply to my faith and fitness focus? What drives me to succeed? What skills does it take for me to do what other people find unappealing?

It was fun to catch myself smiling as I realized my skill set and how much I do delight in the details. I simply love meeting new people—or connecting with familiar friends—and noting the details of their lives. Their favorite foods, favorite flavors, places they wish to visit, you name it: I like to remember. When the opportunity presents itself, I like to follow up with a note or keepsake related to their favorite things. It works well and fits me, because my hobby is gift-giving. Selecting a gift that is meaningful for someone else is super fun and easy for me. I love it.

The ability to catch on quickly, remember the finite details, and take action on all the subtle cues and desires works well for a professional fundraiser and business owner. What I recently discovered is that the origin of my talent and skill set is God. I believe He is pleased with my attention to detail. I never, ever acknowledged that before this year. Remembering the details and giving back is a core component of my identity and, the more I realized that, the more it made sense to me that a work environment built around nonstop giving of time, talent, and funds works for me.

I knew I needed to find new ways to give during my lemon-parade year. Recipes were puzzle pieces for me, as I hadn't really invested time or attention in cooking or baking before this time. I discovered joy in baking and giving homemade desserts and treats to Jim, neighbors, and church friends.

I discovered that running was a form of giving for me, too. If I put in the training time, I could give all my fitness potential to race day. I learned to love the way runners support each other on the course. During a Memorial Day race, I was coming up behind a woman who was running out of power at mile marker two. I encouraged her as we ran, and she crossed the finish line with me. I achieved a new personal record that day and made a new friend. I was fulfilling multiple goals during the race. I even felt my recruiter spirit dancing as I engaged that runner and brought her to the finish line with me. My identity was growing. My faith and fitness combo was working.

Four months later, in Milford Township, a man encouraged me at mile marker two. He said, "You can do it." I like to think of these little exchanges as gifts or lemon zest. These short phrases benefit the giver *and* the receiver. It takes minimal effort and reaps huge rewards. God smiles when we are good to each other. Lemon zest is an element of surprise that changes the flavor of any given day. As I learned to trust and listen for God as a first step, life surprised me more often. Beautiful things would happen daily.

Blessed by pastors, biblical scholars, and Bible-study friends, I learned that faith isn't about pushing harder; it is about opening wider. The first time I heard a friend say that God is near the brokenhearted, I thought of the morning Fran found me in the swimming pool. She found me on one of my most broken days, feeling vulnerable and empty. Through her, I was feeling God's mercy and learning that He knows how this story goes. He has the script, and it is written. I am to follow and obey. My eyes were wide open for clues.

Puzzle pieces appeared everywhere for me. One day at a friend's office in Dexter, I joyfully reached into a large, ceramic bowl full of assorted puzzle pieces. Each piece had an illustration on one side and a word that was meant especially for you on the other side. I reached in, stirred up the bowl and, with every ounce of my optimistic energy, pulled out a blank piece. I was mega disappointed and sad. Blank was not a comfort to me. Blank felt empty. I looked at Marianne and said, "Mine is blank." She said, "No, it isn't blank—it's white space." I kept getting bold reminders to adjust my perspective from loss to potential.

White space continued to surprise me. I felt God working with me in the white space. He needed me to learn to accept His love and seek possibility with Him. It took time for me to see the white space as room for Him to work with me and through me. I knew the reason I was ultra-sensitive to the blank puzzle piece. Marianne didn't at first. I'd taken my résumé to a University of Michigan development career-chat open house on a cold, January evening. I listened to the speakers, and I looked for my niche, my next fit, my next team. At one point in the evening, I took my résumé to a table and, much like speed-dating a person, reviewed it for ninety seconds. This was only the second time my résumé was out and about since I graduated from college in 1983. Needless to say, I was a bit intimidated and uneasy. The human-resources woman glanced at my résumé in the allotted time and said, "Obviously, you have great experience, and I think it is wonderful you are here tonight as a senior-level professional. I do need to tell you that your résumé would be immediately dismissed due to lack of white space."

Here I was in my seat, speed-dating my résumé and thinking I should have added one or two more significant accomplishments, and instead my career is dismissed due to lack of white space. She said there was too much crammed on this one page. All I could do was remain composed and tell her the truth. I said, "Thank you for telling me. It seems my life has been lacking white space." I walked out to the curb, caught my breath, and realized I had just learned a lot more than I bargained for in those ninety seconds. Not sure if that open house was more lemon zest or lemon pith. It was a lemon lesson learned.

Lack of white space never seemed to be a problem when I was working with the American Cancer Society. When your days are full of creating hope and progress on something as rotten as cancer, white space just wasn't a priority. Doing more was my priority. Nonprofit work was the core of our family life. It was full, and we felt good about it. So many times I recalled hearing Jess say, "My parents save lives." It stuck. I liked it.

As I listened to Sunday church sermons, learned in my women's Bible-study group, read in my daily devotional books, I realized an element I was lacking was a daily, conversational relationship with God. Raised Catholic, I believe in the Father, the Son, the Holy Spirit. I had found some comfort in the rituals of church over the years. I prayed my memorized prayers. I believed, but I need more action. More visual cues.

One morning after swimming, I decided to put God in my cell phone contact list. I loved the idea, so I did it. I needed to see His name when scrolling through looking for contacts, numbers, or emails. I needed to establish the habit of calling Him first. Next I thought of it in more practical terms: in an accident situation, if the police were ever to scroll through my contact list and look for the important names highlighted in red. They will find my sister, our daughter, and my husband. I like the idea of them scrolling past God, too. That simple action altered my ability to lean on God. To turn to him and think of him as a resource. It is good to put God in your contact list.

I also wrote His name in my paper address book. The one I keep for Christmas cards. I felt comfort in doing this, thinking about how someday when I am long gone, Jess will be flipping through to find a random relative's mailing address. I want her to laugh out loud and think, *Mum must have sent Jesus a birthday card. Go, Mum!*

God wants us to lean on Him every day. His Word teaches us to focus on Him for support and love. That one threw me for a loop, because I had always worked hard on being self-sufficient and strong enough to get the job done. I am now a leaner, and that requires daily practice and prayer. The great news is that leaning on God takes the load off you. I found that practicing running and leaning on God isn't easy, but it is doable.

Pacing my expectations was another area in which studying faith and fitness at the same time worked well. I couldn't drop fifty pounds in a month or even six. And I couldn't change my relationship with God from religion to relationship with the flip of a switch either. But with persistence and humor, I made progress every day. Humor worked best for both lesson plans. One day I was buzzing page by page through a magazine on nutrition, and what caught my eye was this headline: Understanding the benefits of eating an apple a day versus eating seven all at once. I was starting to get it. Just because something is good for you doesn't mean you can have large quantities of it. Too much of a good thing isn't always better. I learned to respect that running was best if I limited my runs to three or four days per week. Just because a run feels good doesn't mean you can start doing it every day as a newbie.

Learning requires connections, and mine were coming in white spaces, short phrases, and humor. It was all starting to click. I knew my sabbatical year was an investment and that I would make lemonade out of every single brilliant idea. Making good choices and arranging my priorities were the objectives each day. I used proven strategies of business and applied them to life goals. I started to understand that gaining fifty pounds was the result of a series of small compromises. I lost track and ate as if there were no consequences. I learned that food is fuel. That choices need to be conscious. I started to ask myself better questions about food choices. Just like in a one-on-one meeting with a valuable staff person. Ask yourself with care and concern: Do you want to eat a whole pizza, or do you want to be able to run and fit into clothes that feel good and fit right? I leaned on God, and I learned by studying that faith is belief in action—and so is fitness. The body does follow once the mind commits. Discipline and sacrifice are required, but the formula is simple to apply.

Intentional rest is also a key to successful training. I had to learn to respect the rest day, which is the one day during the week that you don't work out. You will need to plan it, protect it, and rest with appreciation for the other six days. I learned to be thankful for the difference it makes. If the rest day is hard for you, focus on how much better you will perform the day after. The best run of the week for me was the one after the rest day. The rest day is like a savings account for energy.

As I was learning to run, a neighbor let me borrow Danny Dreyer's book titled *Chi Running*. With the help of his book, I learned to listen to my body as I run. I loved helpful hints, such as holding your hands as if you are carrying a butterfly when you run. That image helps me each time I run to keep my hands soft and relaxed. Dreyer says that balance doesn't always mean equal balance. It means that in order for something to increase, something else has to decrease, and vice versa. I was learning about life while learning to run.

Balance was important to me yet something just out of my reach for years. I had been striving for balance as long as I could remember. When I learned balance was important to runners, I was hooked. Cheri, from my gym, met with me briefly one day after I had run my first four 5k events. She was a lifelong runner, marathon competitor, and international award winner, yet she gave me such clear, simple, beginner advice. She told me runners need a strong core and balance. She encouraged me to keep up my training and add seven core exercises. I am grateful that she didn't pile on her years of experience and wisdom. Her knowledge was evident, and in her simplistic approach she enabled me to simply own my training and own my runs. Thanks to her I've consistently improved my pace and am injury free. My original strengthening exercises are listed for you in Appendix Three.

Registering for 5k races, especially timed ones, worked well for me. I needed competitive targets to stay on track and build fellowship and fun into my running routine. Jess was my coach when it came to race-day fun and memorabilia. I highly recommend race days with friends. It gives a boost to your training routine. It transforms the personal discipline of running into a social experience. Races are motivators because you see people who are lifelong runners and people who are newbies pushing themselves to compete. It's a mob of people running their own race. You remember the people, the faces, the temperature, your pace, the spots where you wanted to walk, and the spots at which you encouraged others. It is beautiful and simple with lots of white space. I lean on God when I race. My best race mantra is my best prayer: Father, Son, Holy Spirit, help me.

My lemon parade is full of determined people. I have a team. I realized in the first ninety days that I was not alone, so there was no need to fear being alone. My tribe is strong. My tribe believes.

My first 5k day arrived. Jess had team shirts made with a creative nickname on the back. All thirteen team members had a number on their backs specific to a family memory. The shirts were symbols of love and affirmation that none of us was alone. The team shirts being given as gifts is an example of the tangible ways I learned the glory of God. I never told Jess of my fear of being alone once my work team was gone, yet that fear was nonetheless diminished by her act of thoughtful kindness. So here I was thinking faith and fitness would be about learning to pray and losing weight, but early in my sabbatical year I became aware that the white space of my life would make room for simple acts of kindness that showed me love endures. God is good all the time.

My first 5k race was planned for Thanksgiving morning 2013, strategically timed to come twelve weeks after my training started. It was the annual holiday Turkey Trot in downtown Ann Arbor at sunrise. A frigid morning of twenty-three degrees, sharp wind from the north, and snow flurries that accumulated. It was the kind of first snow that seems remarkably beautiful yet unbelievable. Two of my nephews showed up in shorts for the race. But no one complained about the weather. Some of my team members had four layers of cold gear on and their knit face mask pulled down to their chin. Our sweet neighbor boy, with his two little eyes peeping out of his ski mask kept asking me why we were running in the snow. Inside our hearts, my team had a resounding spirit of can-do, warmth, and love.

All of my *Run Your Butt Off* training from the *Runner's World* book had been on a treadmill at the gym. Using the twelve-week program, I went from stepping on a treadmill for the very first time September 1 to the Thanksgiving Turkey Trot with only three practice runs outside. I am still surprised that, even after one full year of running, the first mile of each run is hard. I keep thinking it will get easier, but my expectations are adjusting, and I'm learning to love the reminder that if this were easy, everyone would do it. Sometimes I laugh to myself thinking how full our subdivision streets would be early in the morning if running were easy.

Not to burst anyone's training bubble, but believe me. Running outside is very different than running on the treadmill. I am not sure I would startle people by describing it as harder, exactly. But it most definitely is different. The first time I ran outside, I fully expected the experience to feel the same. Maybe that was naïve, but how could I have known any different? Jess was good about telling me a few weeks before the race to try it outside. I finally listened, and when I tried it I could run only two blocks. I felt out of breath and like my feet were lead stones. That felt like a setback, but I was determined to run the Turkey Trot with my team.

A recurring funny thing about race days is that I still feel nervous at the starting line. I've learned to enjoy the nervous feeling and take it as a cue that my mind, body, and spirit know a test is coming. I believe I can run a strong race because I train. I pray. I use all the skills of my lemon-parade year. Running 5ks has become a combination of celebration and praise-God days for me. I am aware that studying faith and fitness as simultaneous challenges works for my personality. I hope it works for you and your team too.

Each month my weight has dropped. Some months it hasn't been much, but it has always decreased, and my finish times have steadily decreased, too. Right-sizing my body weight and tracking race results provides me the measurable feedback I need. My race results are in Appendix Four.

My lemon-parade year was hard work, on purpose, with purpose. Mission statements do come to life for a big business and for a big life. I know my vocation is to be of service to a compelling mission and people. We have the potential within to positively influence one another on a daily basis.

Lemon Zest

✓ Seizing the opportunity to own your time is essential to lemon-parade success.

✓ Goal achievement is a way to glorify God.

✓ Once your mind decides to lead the way, your body will follow.

✓ You can learn to translate work-goal accomplishment into personal-goal accomplishment.

✓ Faith isn't about pushing harder; it is about opening wider.

✓ You have the ability to lead your own faith and fitness development step by step.

✓ Lemon-parade thoughts focus on accepting today, moving on, and celebrating what will be next.

✓ Too much clutter doesn't leave enough white space for growth and improvement.

✓ Balance and core strength are necessary for learning to run.

✓ Changing habits is hard work but rewarding when you push through the slumps.

✓ Add your own:

_____

✓ Add your own:

_____

Chapter Five:
Beacon of Health

Reading short phrases in running magazines really helped me in the middle of my training. One concept that stuck in my brain is the belief that if you do the training, the run is in you. All you have to do on race day is relax and let it out. I also reminded myself while running that becoming strong and fit was my full-time job at that moment. It really helped me to think of running and improving myself as my job. I knew how to be successful at work, so my brain easily accepted that fact, and my body always followed.

For me, running wasn't a hobby, nor just a way to lose fifty pounds; it was my challenge and my focus area. It was something I planned to excel at from day one. Because my vision was so clear, and I tracked my training in a simple log, my time and pace improved at most races. I believe linking running to something I was already good at (work-goal achievement) made it doable and familiar to me.

Learning to relax and trust the training were meaningful lessons for both my faith and fitness curriculum. My personal transformation from a woman who felt responsible to push harder and work harder to a confident Christian athlete was not easy, but it was doable. I linked business-success patterns and habits to faith and fitness. I am convinced that if you use a pattern that is familiar to you and plug in the new knowledge and habits, then success happens over time with discipline and courage. Toward the end of my lemon-parade year, I gained confidence in the skills I needed to be competitive and proficient in my new passions. To help me remain focused on what is possible, rather than on what is fearful or unsettling, I learned to quickly recall the good habits that had changed my physical condition. I deliberately changed my thoughts over the course of the year, which changed my habits, which changed my perspective and outcomes. I learned to practice relaxing and quieting my mind in the pool at the gym. The small, warm pool was the first place I had to answer the tough question, "What do you do?"

The pool became a place where I felt closer to God. If I showed up, He did too. I believe He will meet you wherever you are when you set aside the time and focus on hearing His voice. Over twelve months, I tried yoga and Pilates, and I am grateful I eventually found my space to pause and communicate with God in the pool. I've heard walking in parks or on trails can spark this quiet, safe place for people. Now I understand. It doesn't matter what the place is for you; what matters most is that you discover it. He will show up. He always does.

I encourage you to make it a priority to find this space for yourself and then go there. Some people may refer to this time and space as meditation. I also learned to count my blessings in the sauna. Learning to enjoy the sauna took me some time because I couldn't understand the benefit of feeling so hot and sweaty just lying there. It was a place for me to practice relaxation and the discipline to just be still and trust ancient wisdom.

One day in the sauna at the gym, a woman who seemed agitated and uneasy asked me what I thought about while in the sauna. We had stepped out one after the other and were heading to the showers. I told her I count my blessings and won't let my mind wander from that thought process. She said she was in the same sauna for the same eight minutes, and all she did was process her worries and her anger toward her teenager. There we were, two women, same sauna, roughly the same age, but running two completely different lists through our minds. This innocent interaction was a blessing and an example to me of intentional faith and fitness. It isn't necessarily the time, space, or equipment that makes the lemon parade work; it is seizing the opportunity to invest your time to do good for yourself. Everything takes time, even running lists through your brain in the quiet space of a public sauna. Being peaceful or angry is a choice. Choose wisely and practice forgiveness—it frees your brain to nurture your body and soul.

It still surprises me how the pool (of all places) became peaceful to my heart and soul, because in the beginning it was where I felt especially lonely and vulnerable. But week after week, I confronted the lonely space and took responsibility for my thought processes and feelings. I used personal discipline to change my thinking and started to intentionally open my mind and, eventually, my heart there. Once I could do it there as a pattern, I could do it anywhere. I was onto something. Conquering fear to accomplish personal goals was a workout.

Eventually, my best conversations with God took place in the pool. I learned that He was always available; it was me who needed to alter my openness in order to build a relationship with Him. One morning toward the end of my lemon-parade year, I was praying with my arms comfortably crossed at the edge of the pool. Happy as a clam, with my legs kicking and dangling, I gently propped my chin on my hands and let my mind open to listening and focusing on grateful thoughts. When I opened my eyes after prayer, I was startled to see a man from the lap pool across the glass divide staring at my face and chuckling. He said he was doing his laps when my face caught his eye, and he had to stop. He said, "I was sure you had fallen asleep. I've never seen an awake face look that peaceful." I just smiled and assured him I hadn't been asleep.

I was delighted to know that I was looking peaceful on the outside, because I felt such peace on the inside. Deeply, spiritually, physically peaceful and well. I invested the time to discover this space, and it will serve me well each day for the next fifty years.

Developing the habit of prayer became an intentional component of my faith and fitness training. I needed to prioritize time for prayer similar to time for physical fitness. Time invested in prayer and personal conversation with God on a daily basis was a new habit for me.

I started to enjoy the regular feeling of being healthy, fit, and tone. I felt as if my body, heart, and soul were being transformed. I knew I was on the right path, at the right time in my life. I remember the emotions that washed over me the first day I felt 100-percent content. I discovered my peace: faith and fitness are my pillars to get there. That simple formula works for me. It took a science-experiment mindset to get there, courage in the middle, and acceptance at the end. It was worth every good choice and purposeful decision, step by step.

In January 2014, Jess invited me to run the Atlanta Hot Chocolate 5k with her. I accepted her invitation for so many mother-daughter reasons: Time alone with her. Just the two of us in a Southern city, which I hoped would be a little warmer than Michigan is that time of year. Fitness was providing a fresh, new bond with Jess. I loved her approach to encouraging and supporting me. It was a chance for me to be the student and for her to be the teacher. Jess was always good with honest running feedback, but she never overwhelmed me with her knowledge or expectation for running.

It was a chilly weekend in Atlanta, and at 5:45 a.m. when we left our hotel near Olympic Park, it was a very dark and windy twenty-three degrees. I had faithfully trained on the treadmill at the gym since the Holiday Hustle 5k in early December, and I felt I'd be able to keep up the pace and not take walking breaks at all during this race. What took my newbie race heart by surprise was the congested start, when twenty-three thousand runners are all up and running on a winter Saturday in Atlanta. It was crowded, and that really slowed me down at the start. It was my fourth 5k, and there were two small hills on the course. I walked twice to catch my breath.

Jess stayed by me the whole race, even though I knew she could run faster. I wanted to finish strong, and I did push to my best pace at the finish. It was the first time I noticed a three-mile marker on the route, and my brain thought *go hard*, for one-tenth of a mile, just to feel the rush. I did. It was great to see Jess's expression at the finish line. She said, "Where did that come from?" I said, "I wanted to finish strong. I didn't want to walk at all this race and was bummed to have to walk twice on the hills. I didn't expect the run to still be hard." Jess, in her firm and direct way, simply looked at me and said, "It's always hard. You just get used to it." *What the heck am I going to do with that new information?* I thought to myself on the long walk back to the shuttle bus, back to the parking lot, back to the hotel. *Running is always going to be hard? I am going to get used to hard?* I learned that if I considered running the hard part of my day, I could get that done and conquer the rest of the day. Consider running done and consider the rest easy.

Lemon Zest

- ✓ If you do the training, the run is in you.
- ✓ Learn to relax and trust the training for both faith- and fitness-development success.
- ✓ Change your thoughts. This will change your habits, which will change your perspective and outcome.
- ✓ Running never stops being hard, but you will get used to it.
- ✓ Find a place where you feel close to God.
- ✓ Conquer fear to accomplish personal goals.
- ✓ Invest time every day talking with God.
- ✓ Add your own:

_____

- ✓ Add your own:

_____

Chapter Six:
Lemon Zest

The faith and fitness work during my lemon-parade year felt valuable and precious. It dawned on me that if I do live to be one hundred years old, this sabbatical year was only one percent of my entire life. I smiled to think about the return on this incredible investment.

Reflecting on all the conversations I'd shared with cancer survivors, I kept remembering how their first year of treatment impacted their lives, their perspectives, and their families. I felt like a portion of my peace with my lemon-parade year was a tribute to their life lessons.

Cancer always seemed to steal people's innocence. Cancer was rude. I never wanted to be rude. Cancer survivors always found a way to vividly explain their loss of freedom. I knew so many that felt their vitality, time, options, and energy were stolen in the night. I had been a great student, and they had been thoughtful teachers. I was determined not to squander a minute of my lemon-parade year. I learned that a year of wellness, or a year of illness, shifts your perspective and priorities. Illness may not be a lifestyle by choice, but wellness must be.

Every time I took my next step of physical and spiritual wellness, God met me. He always sent a caring, faith-filled companion to take my hand, like Fran did in the pool. Her short phrase, "You'll be fine," became an empowering mantra for me. After months of developing new habits, I learned I wouldn't be fine by working harder; I would be fine when I prayed first and expected the best. Developing faith and fitness strengths as parallel studies worked for me because they both required effort and knowledge. Life is competitive, but it is not a contest. Our trust in God is the prize.

41

Techniques and tips helped me learn to run. In one issue of a running magazine, I read a tip to control your breathing while learning to run. The article mentioned the benefits of inhaling for two beats and exhaling for three beats. That seemed backward to me, based on my push-hard, do-more, work-harder mindset. I would have thought I should breathe in more. Do more. Take in more air.

The main point of the short article was that the more you exhale, the more expanded your lungs are, and the deeper your lungs can take in air during the next two breaths. Making your lungs more efficient by exhaling for an extra beat was a lightning bolt of new knowledge to my brain. So I started to focus on my breathing at the beginning, middle, and end of each run. I practiced like a trooper. Two in, three out. It didn't feel normal at first, but it worked. I kept applying new knowledge of faith and fitness to my life each day. Even if it didn't make sense or feel normal. I had to practice, believe, and trust. I was transforming every part of my life with new thoughts and patterns.

Some days, when I least expected it, transforming felt awkward and emotional. For example, I went to a networking coffee chat one summer morning in Ann Arbor. I felt appropriately prepared and ready to contribute to the fundraising conversation. But, once I arrived I had an immediate fish-out-of-water feeling. I had gone to the coffee chat prepared to find new connections, discover a few missing puzzle pieces, possibly stumble upon the steps to my next career. Instead I learned a priceless, hard lesson.

Here I was, nine months into the lemon-parade year, and I was still learning lessons and forming new habits. What zapped me during the networking coffee chat was one young woman who was describing her passion for her nonprofit agency and her daily responsibilities there. As I listened, I felt that familiar tug of how great it feels to make a difference. I was listening with my full attention and admiration. I was sharing in her stories of affecting lives and raising dollars to make the mission work.

Then she folded her arms, sat up straighter, got my full attention and said, "I have no life. All I do is work." She was proud of it. That statement rolled off her lips like an anthem for serving nonprofits. I knew what she meant, but instead of chiming in and supporting that concept, I stopped. I caught myself for the first time wanting to share in public the importance of having a life too. Even for an hour, a day, a month, or a year. It is necessary to stop and plan and do your life.

The coffee was great, and the people were nice, but I ended up driving home that morning with salty tears of confusion. The good news was I called a super-cool woman when I got back to my desk that morning, and she quickly reminded me that sometimes the greatest blessings are when we learn what we don't want. I believe my stinging tears that morning were for all the faith and fitness opportunities I'd let slip away by being busy.

The gift I received from the woman at the coffee chat was complex. Part of me had such compassion for her; part of me knew exactly what she meant and how okay she was with her life. She had no life and really excelled at it.

The morning after the coffee chat, I needed to celebrate that huge aha with a new experiment. I decided to experiment with learning to put off doing a task—any simple thing—until tomorrow. I realize this might sound odd, but I really enjoy doing my work tasks, on time, right now. I decided to purposefully spend three days consciously trying to pick tasks that could wait. It was comical and hard for me.

I wasn't picking items like prayer or running, but tasks like paying bills or opening the mail. I wanted to test the idea of letting some non–time sensitive responsibilities just simmer for one day. It took discipline for me not to push to get it all done in the moment. Getting things done swiftly was a skill that worked well with business and project management. Learning to let some tasks wait was step one for me to experience the feeling of letting go. In order to lean on God, I had to practice letting go of little things, then bigger things. It was another process for me to learn step by step. Let it go until tomorrow, then let it go. I could practice with minor tasks, and then apply them to large life concepts. This was how I learned to lean on and trust in God's help and love in my life. I didn't flip a switch. Not at all. I practiced and had to intentionally try hard.

Keeping up with all the tasks at once had become a bit of an obsession. The more there was to do, the more I seemed to be able to do. My capacity for volume fed my desire to overachieve, and it felt very natural. To alter that pattern, I started with small tasks, and then started to practice with actions and choices. Day-to-day choices like not raising my hand for a volunteer opportunity at church, or not offering to host a meeting or assemble a packet. In order to make more room in my calendar for my life, I had to practice not always being "the one." I learned that just because you can, doesn't mean you should.

During my experiment, I started to learn that small ways to build a healthier life included efforts to keep my calendar lighter. I had to practice making careful decisions. It helps to think of your time as a finite resource worth protecting. Making good choices is relevant to exercise, nutrition, and calendar clutter. Some days I would even look at what I could delete from my calendar, and I noticed it didn't stop forward progress. I felt lighter on my calendar, and that started to show up on the scale. Being loaded down mentally over the last eleven years translated, for me, to being loaded down physically.

Small adjustments in the calendar made a huge difference in where I could invest my time and energy. Calendar management was key to faith and fitness development for me. The fact that we all get the same twenty-four hours is a stabilizer and common denominator. How we use the hours is up to us. God created us to have free will, and that can be a curse or a blessing. Carefully plan your time and monitor where it can be conserved. It is a similar strategy to that used for currency. An hour saved is an hour earned for your top priorities. The return on investment is brilliant when the results are what you truly crave.

Another great lesson from the calendar clearing experiment and doing less was that when you don't do it, someone else has a chance to try. As one of my mentors always says, "Know your role and do it well." What took me a while to realize and practice is the fact that you need only to do your own role.

Similarly, like eliminating unhealthy habits from my calendar one day at a time, I had to work to eliminate bad eating habits. Just because you think of pizza doesn't mean you have to eat one. Even after a full year of lemon-parade discipline when it comes to eating habits, I think of pizza at least once a day. I remember it fondly and move on.

In the past, if I thought of pizza, I ate it. I think I thought of eating as a to-do list. Think—do—eat. That seems odd and wrong to me now, but when I was eating unconsciously, it was aligned like all other business tasks. Think of it. Do it. Move on. Consider it accomplished. The problem was too many bad choices that felt okay in the moment. Fattening foods that weren't consumed in huge amounts but nonetheless without strategy or forethought. Food was a means to keep the production level high. Ultimately, that kept the scale and the pants size high, too.

Now when I think of pizza, or any other food that becomes a craving, I satisfy that craving in another way. The best way I have found to resist cravings is to eat often and to exercise every day. And to transfer the craving to activities, instead of letting the to-do thought be food-centric. These days, I crave running with Jess, learning more and loving life, sharing healthy outdoor activities with family and friends. I crave quiet prayer time with God. I crave my next challenge because I know I am never alone, and with His partnership all is possible. I am not afraid. I may still feel fear, but I have developed the habit and patterns to refocus my feelings into faith-filled actions.

In order to achieve my top priorities, I had to learn to transform my habits, my choices, and my cravings. It is hard, but doable. Some comfort foods and beverages were harder to break up with than others. I did stop eating chunks of Kraft cheddar cheese, Triscuits, and pinot grigio. That trio of comfort was a crutch for me.

I learned to enjoy and crave the feeling of making healthier choices. I started to think of what I ate each day as a solid, strategic business decision. Faith and fitness development was my job, and I had to manage the bottom line and be accountable. Choice by choice, it worked. In the middle of a 5k if I felt off pace I would simply remind myself that this is my job, and I am good at my work. That triggered my can-do spirit, and I always finished strong. It is key to find out how your brain and inner voice are wired, then go with your strengths and achieve your priorities. Simple and effective strategy worked every time for me.

People who noticed my weight loss would frequently ask the same question. What program did you use? Every time they asked the question, they immediately answered with Weight Watchers before I could say a word. I guess that is a great endorsement for Weight Watchers. I didn't use Weight Watchers and never even considered a packaged weight-loss program.

From day one, I knew faith and fitness were my focus and my business. I started with a health assessment at the gym. Just like in business, I needed to know the condition of the materials (in this case my physical strength and stamina) to build a solid plan for improvement. My initial assessment was easy, private, and provided at no additional cost to me. With a fitness specialist named Brian, I was fired up to gather the data and improve. He was calm, confident, and relaxed about first steps. Brian did all ten assessments for me, including percentage of body fat, push-ups, VO2, and blood pressure, which are found in Appendix Two. During the assessment, he wasn't ever critical, just honest and soft-spoken. I told him my goals to run my first 5k by Thanksgiving and to drop fifty pounds in fifty weeks.

I asked Brian to explain to me what behaviors I needed to change in order to lose fifty pounds in fifty weeks. He told me to consume five hundred fewer calories a day and be active at least five days a week. There I sat. An eager, optimistic overachiever thinking to myself, *I need to know what five hundred calories looks like*. I am a visual learner. I asked more specific questions and, much to my surprise, he told me five hundred calories is that bowl of chips you eat at night. How did he know I loved a bowl of chips at night? I even had a special bowl just for chips at night. I had a chip and chip-bowl relationship and bad habit. Farewell chips at night.

Brian told me I could also think about one slice of bread instead of two on a sandwich. His last suggestion was to eat more vegetables and less pasta. I had three strategies, and I was good to go. I am good with short phrases and minimal instruction. Business strategy 101. Grasp the concept, and make it happen. It was simple, and I could take immediate action. Think of it in terms of this scenario: You find out something incredibly simple and easy to fix is negatively impacting your customers' experience or your marketing plan. The issue is costing your company revenue and future gain. You would fix it right then. Same plan, different context. My program was cutting five hundred calories every day and exercising six days a week. I planned one rest day each week, and it always benefitted me.

After I did the treadmill test, Brian told me my heart was strong enough for a 5k right then. That stuck with me through the months I tried to learn to run on the treadmill using the *Run Your Butt Off* book and training plan. And his words did spring to mind the first time I tried to run outside in October. The difference was a real surprise. I texted Jess, "I can do thirty minutes on the treadmill. I can't do two minutes outside." She texted back, "Yeah, it's different." Jess was great that way. She never panicked or overcompensated for my shocked responses to running setbacks.

I knew my heart was physically strong enough to run a 5k from the assessment with Brian. I knew my brain was strong enough to run a 5k, because I had a strong yearning to experience running beside Jess. The body will follow where the brain leads. Knowing my heart was strong enough even though I had never stepped on a treadmill led me to believe I was a runner who had just missed my calling and was starting late. So many of my nieces and nephews are great runners, I even believed it was hereditary. Running was an untapped ability, and I was a determined voyager.

What I didn't know was that my heart wasn't spiritually tuned up to exercise at all. The running articles I read didn't explain the nagging gremlins that sit on your shoulders shouting that you look wrong, or look slow, or that you haven't been training enough. Humor and prayer were blessings on the days when running didn't come easily. I liked the mental training it took to push the mind-game gremlins back to their place, especially during races but also on training days. It sounds so cliché but is so true. Don't think about it, just put your shoes on and go. The gremlins aren't strong, but they are persistent. They cave every time. Once during a race, I laughed out loud because the gremlins were extra negative, yet my Garmin watch showed my pace to be setting a new personal record. Gremlins are evil and aggravating, but they don't run the show. You do, always and in all ways. My running mantra, for when my tank feels empty, is simple: Father, Son, Holy Spirit, help me. I learned to ask for God's help while running because I really needed it. That practice of asking for help soon became a habit. I believe God likes that I ask. He always hears me.

I needed prayer to run, and I needed running to get my body moving and get the weight off. My brain was the ultimate drum major leading my lemon parade. I managed my weight loss and running program like a business. I am good at business. I purposefully attached new habits to familiar patterns. Try to delight in the details of your faith and fitness experience just like any other strategic plan. Invest your time wisely and keep the mission top of mind all day, every day. It works.

Food became fuel for running. Period. That simple strategy made my food choices easy. I started to read one or two running magazines. I needed to learn the lingo and absorb the lifestyle. I wanted it. Good food choices became huge motivators for me. Do I miss pizza? Sure. But not as much as I like buying size 8 capris and business suits.

Ultimately, dropping the weight and training to run has been a choice-by-choice, day-by-day process. The discipline to live an obedient and prayerful daily life complements a fitness plan like a hand in a glove. I can't imagine tackling one without the other. Looking at my data at the end of my lemon-parade year was the best annual review of my career. I've been fortunate to work with some remarkable supervisors and benefitted from their careful, observant annual reviews. It feels great to know that my personal review of my sabbatical year is on target for all of my top five goals.

The joy of faith and fitness peaks as I share precious race experiences with my daughter; her husband, Dan; and my sister, Connie. At the June race in Charlevoix, Dan ran his first marathon and qualified for Boston 2015. Having a photo with all three of us with our medals is a great gift. Me with my 5k medal, Jess with her 10k, and Dan with his first marathon medal. I achieved the ability to participate by making better daily choices. I realized after the Charlevoix experience that my physical potential was buried in my bad habits and disbelief for years. What a life-changing discovery my lemon parade has been. I believe I gained more than I lost. The gain was in wisdom, self-identity, and trust. One of the blessings that I can cherish most from my lemon-parade year is that I never felt alone. I found comrades everywhere I turned. From the gym, to church, to casual acquaintances along the 5k routes. I learned that heartbroken is okay and sometimes even necessary. I discovered that healing is possible, and peace of mind is real.

I learned to respect sleep like never before, too. Solid, deep sleep seemed to be essential to my weight loss. There was a point at which my sleep became deeper due in part to exercise, but I also think my faith and trust in God to know the plan helped put my brain to rest. It felt as though my body and mind adjusted over time. They became less swollen and leaner as the chronic exhaustion vanished.

My lemon-parade year felt like a science experiment in the beginning, a treasure hunt in the middle, and a mission trip at the end. I can honestly report that every day of my lemon parade, I directed my energy and focus forward. I met an intuitive, straightforward woman just as my sabbatical year ended. She promptly asked me, "Are you a brand-new person?" My response was quick and sincere, "I am not a brand-new person. I am the best version of my former self."

From that moment on, I realized that personal transformation doesn't require leaving yourself behind or checking your history at the starting line. From my experience, it is a process of refining and defining as you learn in real time, with your whole heart and brain in sync. The essential elements are surprisingly simple and basic. Keep learning, stay optimistic, and intentionally connect with people who will cheer for you and support your lemon parade.

For me, the ultimate transformation included four phases: Phase one was the woman who had to know the plan. Phase two featured the woman who could function with the discomfort of not knowing the plan. During phase three, the woman blossomed who could accept not knowing. Finally, in phase four the woman learned to appreciate the unknown. I evolved from needing to build the plan by myself to learning to trust that He has the plan. I always knew discipline creates performance. I needed to learn that discipleship creates a lighter load that you never carry alone.

I love my life. I am not finished.

Lemon Zest
- ✓ Wellness is a lifestyle choice, made one decision at a time.
- ✓ Weight loss is the result of a lifestyle change.
- ✓ Life is competitive, but it is not a contest.
- ✓ Eat the right foods often, and exercise six days a week.
- ✓ You have the power to become the best version of yourself.
- ✓ Discipline helps you gain more in perspective than you lose in weight.
- ✓ You can build a plan, work a plan, and love your life with Him.
- ✓ Add your own:

  _____

- ✓ Add your own:

  _____

Appendix One:
My Weight Loss by Date and Pounds

Date	Weight (lbs)	
7.5.13	207	
7.15.13	204	
8.19.13	198.4	
9.20.13	192.6	
10.22.13	190.1	
11.11.13	188.3	
11.29.13	186.1	
12.16.13	184.3	
1.8.14	182.6	
1.20.14	179.3	
2.21.14	175.8	
3.21.14	173.3	
4.14.14	171.8	
5.19.14	170.9	
6.19.14	169.5	Size 8 capris and Size 10 business suit
7.5.14	166.1	41 pounds off
8.19.14	164	
9.15.14	162	My first time stepping on the scale feeling confident that my weight had gone down
10.27.14	160	
11.30.14	157	
Goal	**157**	

Appendix Two:

Fitness Assessment
First Month, Six-month Check-in, and
After One Full Year at Gym

	7/12/13	1/29/14	7/14/14
Resting HR (bpm)	80	60	66
Blood Pressure	134/80	120/70	121/72
% Body Fat	37	35	30.5
Waist (inches)	34.5	32.5	30
Hip (inches)	43	42.25	40
BMI	31.75	27.1	24.5
Grip Strength	L: 57 R: 65	L: 62 R: 62	L: 60 R: 70
Pushups	0	11	19
VO2	35 Average	38 Excellent	38 Excellent
Sit and Reach (inches)	17	28.75	29

Appendix Three:
My Strength Training, Started 11.18.13

Specific goal: To increase strength to improve running

Frequency: Three days per week

Work up to ten minutes of core work starting with seven different exercises at one minute each:

_____ Arm Swings with five-pound weights, thirty seconds per set, do three sets

_____ Lunge forward, push off front foot and tap back knee on ground with light weight, two sets of five, each leg

Fifteen reps of each of these five exercises:

_____ Crunches—cross arms over chest with knees bent and feet on floor

_____ Plank—on toes and elbows, thirty seconds

_____ Bicycle—in a V with legs up and elbows toward knees with hands behind head

_____ Bird dog—right hand pointed out with left leg pointed back, then switch sides

_____ Push-ups on knees—try for five

Appendix Four:
5k Races and Results—
Goal to Complete 20 in 12 Months

Date	Race	Race Partners	Time
Nov. 28, 2013	Ann Arbor Turkey Trot Ann Arbor, MI	Team of 13 family and friends	36:54
Dec. 7, 2013	Dexter Holiday Hustle Dexter, MI	Alone	37:22
Dec. 21, 2013	Ugly Sweater Run National Harbor, MD	Jess	38:05
Jan. 26, 2014	Hot Chocolate Atlanta, GA	Jess	37:41
March 9, 2014	Ann Arbor Shamrocks and Shenanigans Ann Arbor, MI	Alone	35:44
April 6, 2014	Big House U-M Ann Arbor, MI	Dave	33:57
May 10, 2014	Herndon Middle School Herndon, VA	Jess	34:14
May 11, 2014	Reston Mother's Day- 4 miler (longer distance) Reston, VA	Jess	48:00
May 17, 2014	Huron Valley Humane Society Walk and Wag Ypsilanti, MI	Alone	33.46
May 26, 2014	Pinckney Memorial Day Pinckney, MI	Alone	33:00
June 1, 2014	Dexter Ann Arbor Run Ann Arbor, MI	Alone	33:07
June 21, 2014	Charlevoix 5k Charlevoix, MI 3rd Place	Jess	32:20
July 4, 2014	Ann Arbor Firecracker Ann Arbor, MI	Alone	30:52
Aug. 9, 2014	Saline Summerfest Saline, MI	Alone	31:00
Sept. 13, 2014	Kensington Metro Park Milford, MI	Debbie, Dave & Arielle	30:30

Date	Race	Race Partners	Time
Oct. 4, 2014	Bruckelaufe Bridge Run Frankenmuth, MI	Alone	31:03
Oct. 11, 2014	Run Scream Run, Wiard's Orchard Ypsilanti, MI	Jess	30:21
Oct. 25, 2014	Girls on the Run Super Hero Hudson Mills, MI	Hershners and Debbie	30:02
Nov. 8, 2014	Hot Cocoa Classic, Mt. Brighton Brighton, MI 2nd place	Debbie	32:04
Nov. 27, 2014	Turkey Trot Ann Arbor, MI	Coach Hutchins Hershners	28:04

Appendix Five:
Books and Magazines that Supported
My Lemon-Parade Year

The Bible, New International Version
Jesus Calling, daily devotional by Sarah Young
Trusting God Day by Day, devotional by Joyce Meyer
Making Good Habits, Breaking Bad Habits by Joyce Meyer
Run Your Butt Off! by Sarah Lorge Butler with Leslie Bonci and Budd Coates, the *Runner's World* running coach
Chi Running by Danny Dreyer
Touch the Sky! by Eleni Kelakos
Now, Discover Your Strengths by Marcus Buckingham and Donald Clifton
Women's Running magazine
Runner's World magazine

Appendix Six:
Summary of Lemon Zests by Topic

Lemon Zest & Change

Courage in times of change is good.

The good news is that when you get your "What IF" moment, you will know it is the truth.

Life hands people lemons all the time.

Lemon-parade thoughts focus on accepting today, moving on, and celebrating what will be next.

Change your thoughts. This will change your habits, which will change your perspective and outcome.

Personal connection to a valuable mission impacts your life in many different ways.

Life is competitive, but it is not a contest.

You can build a plan, work a plan, and love your life with Him.

Lemon Zest & Determination

Believing in the right stuff requires courage, discretion, and time.

Lemon zest is an element of surprise that changes the flavor of your day.

Every time you stretch, you will go farther, faster.

Planned daily discomfort helps create new habits.

Seizing the opportunity to own your time is essential to lemon-parade success.

Changing habits is hard work but rewarding when you push through the slumps.

Conquer fear to accomplish personal goals.

Your feet point forward for a reason.

Lemon Zest & Faith

Seek and find a source of comfort and peace in your life.

You can recognize your potential in a new Christian friend.

Learn to relax and trust the training for both faith- and fitness-development success.

Find a place where you feel close to God.

Invest time every day talking with God.

Relationships with talented, cool, vibrant people aren't linear; they are full-circle.

Faith isn't about pushing harder; it is about opening wider.

Goal achievement is a way to glorify God.

Lemon Zest & Fitness

Weight loss is the result of a lifestyle change.

Once your mind decides to lead the way, your body will follow.

You have the ability to lead your own faith and fitness development step by step.

Balance and core strength are necessary for learning to run.

If you do the training, the run is in you.

Running never stops being hard, but you will get used to it.

Wellness is a lifestyle choice, made one decision at a time.

Eat the right foods often, and exercise six days a week.

Discipline helps you gain more in perspective than you lose in weight.

Lemon Zest & Opportunity

When life hands you lemons, little things matter.

Each new beginning deserves a parade of some sort.

The day you need it most, your personal mission statement will matter most.

You can learn to translate work-goal accomplishment into personal-goal accomplishment.

Fear can't touch a moving target. —Eleni Kelakos

Not knowing doesn't equal being unsuccessful.

Too much clutter doesn't leave enough white space for growth and improvement.

You have the power to become the best version of yourself.

About the Author

Dear Lisa,
Merry Christmas
2014!
love,
Tami

Tami Rummel is a passionate, goal-oriented professional fundraiser dedicated to making an impact in her community and beyond. She is a graduate of the Michigan State University and a member of the United Methodist Church. Her life has been deeply influenced by successful university coaches, spiritual mentors, and cancer survivors. Favorite hobbies include running, floral design, gift-giving, and volunteer leadership. Rummel resides in Dexter, Michigan, with her husband, Jim; and two noisy Maltese puppies.